STRAIN

WORRY

OVERWHELMED

StReSS

... is what you feel when you are really worried or uncomfortable about something.

PRESSURE

NERVOUS

FEAR

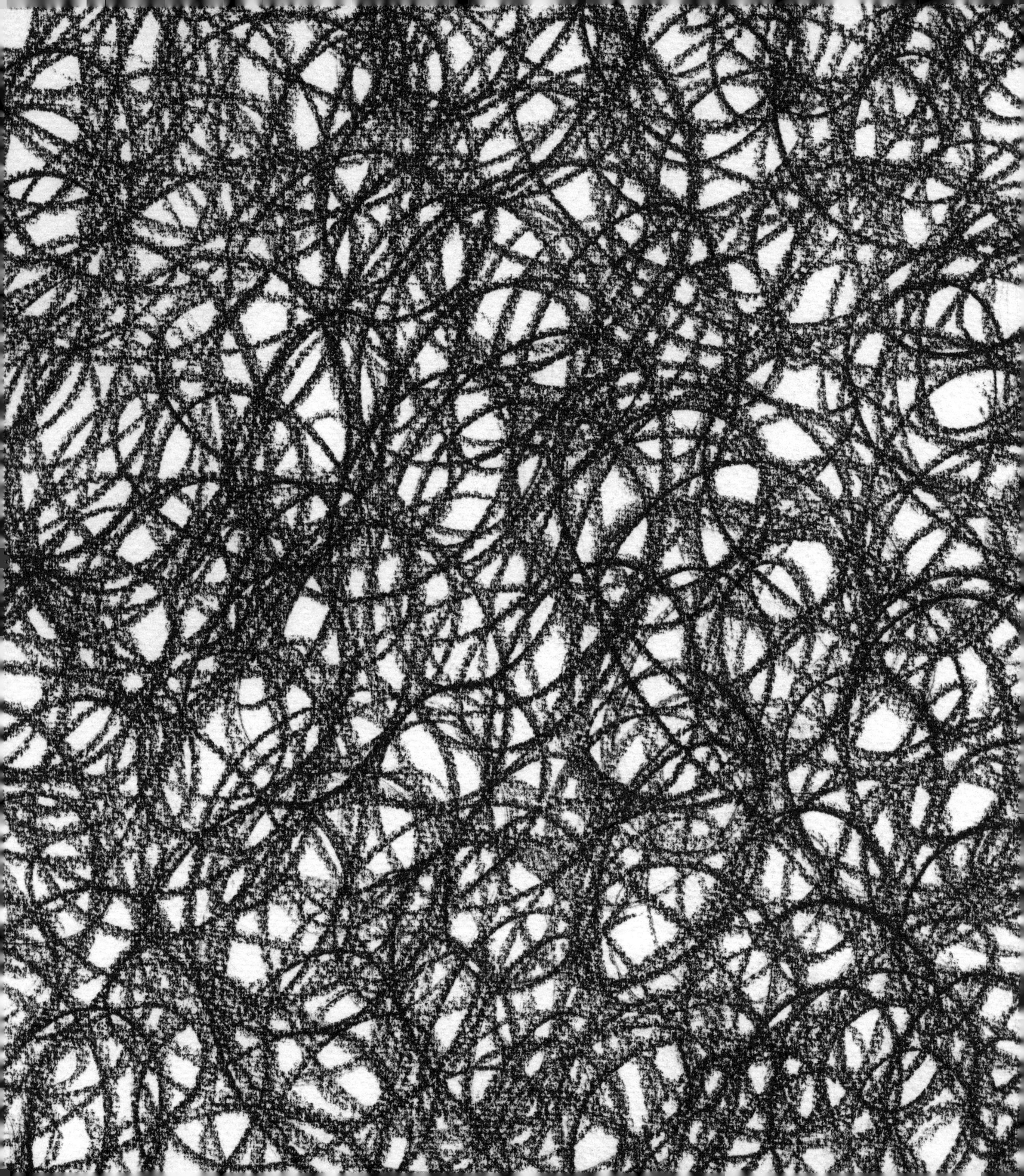

STRESS ANXIETY and ME

written, illustrated & designed by trace moroney

Have you ever heard someone say ...

And have you ever wondered what **stress** actually means?

If you have ever felt so worried about something that you couldn't sleep ... then you may know what it's like to feel stress.

Stress is what I feel when I am really worried
or uncomfortable about something.
It is my body's reaction to pressure or a challenge.

Stress can come from any thing or thought
that makes me feel nervous, frustrated,
uneasy, upset, scared, angry ...
or, sometimes, even excited.

Feeling stress can change how I think,
how I behave, and the choices I make.

1
2
3
4
5

Some things that can make me feel stress are:

HAVING BAD THOUGHTS ABOUT MYSELF

STARTING A NEW SCHOOL

SCARY MOVIES, BOOKS, OR DIGITAL GAMES

PRESSURE TO DO WELL AT SCHOOL OR OTHER ACTIVITIES

SEEING HORRIBLE PICTURES OF VIOLENCE IN THE NEWS OR ON TV

A CHANGE IN MY FAMILY – LIKE DIVORCE, MOVING HOUSE, OR A NEW FAMILY MEMBER

... AND SOMETIMES ... JUST FEELING EXCITED!

PROBLEMS WITH FRIENDS

FEELING LIKE I'M NOT ACCEPTED AND DON'T FIT IN

FEELING UNHAPPY AT SCHOOL

DEATH OR ILLNESS OF A FAMILY MEMBER

FEELING UNHAPPY AT HOME

GOING THROUGH BODY CHANGES

PAIN, INJURY, OR ILLNESS

FEELING SCARED

BEING BULLIED

PARENTS FIGHTING

FEELING UNSAFE

Can you think of other things that make **you** feel stress?

Stress can be good in short bursts ... like
when it gives my body a sudden boost of energy
to make me feel more alert and aware ...
for things like ...
making a speech in front of my class, or
getting ready for a test or competition,
or ... to **run away**

from

danger!

Good stress can help me be aware of dangerous situations and can help push me to get things done.

This type of stress usually goes away quickly after the stress-causing thing has gone.

But bad stress is when stressful feelings last for a long time ... like when I am being bullied, or if a family member is sick or has died, or anything that makes me feel upset and uneasy every day. And ... sometimes I feel stress for no reason at all.

Stress can change the way I feel about myself and others, and how I see the world.

Stress that stays after a stress-causing thing has gone away is sometimes called **anxiety** (how to say it: ang-zy-et-ee).

Most of the time, I don't realise I am feeling stress until my body sends messages to tell me. And sometimes these messages can be **really** confusing!

These are some messages, or things my body may do when it is feeling stress:

wetting the bed
grinding teeth
pain, fever, or rash
headaches
faster heartbeat and breathing
shaky hands
sweaty hands
nightmares

And this is how stress may affect my feelings and behaviour:

Not able to relax

Not able to control emotions

New or growing fears (like feeling scared to be alone, or being scared of the dark)

Temper tantrums

Crying

Don't want to join in (with family, friends, or school activities)

Not able to concentrate

Being quieter than usual

Feeling anxious

New nervous habits (like biting nails or sucking thumb)

Feeling moody

Feeling tired

Trouble remembering things

Feeling clingy (need to be with someone all the time)

Not able to pay attention

Feeling stress is **normal**.
We **all** feel stress at different times about different things, and react in different ways.

What may be stressful for me ...
may not be stressful for you.

Some people seem to cope with stress easily, while others struggle with feeling stress and anxiety ***most of the time***.

Sometimes I feel I can cope ... and other times I feel

OUT OF CONTROL!

When I am feeling stress, I try to remember

THE THINGS I CAN'T CONTROL:

What other people think

What other people say

How other people behave

Mistakes I made in the past

When I get sick

When other people get sick

Anything that happened in the past

When change happens

When someone dies

The weather

Knowing what will happen in the future

When the sun comes up or goes down

… and focus on

THE THINGS I CAN CONTROL:

- My thoughts and behaviours
- Learning from my mistakes
- My effort
- My goals
- Being kind to myself and others
- Who my friends are
- When I ask for help
- The things I love about being Me!
- Taking care of myself
- How I treat people
- Who I love

Here are some things to do to help cope with stress (choose whatever works best for **YOU** or try them all!):

EAT HEALTHY

Having lots of foods and drinks with sugar and fats can stress our bodies. Try to drink lots of water and focus on eating healthy foods (especially vegetables and grains) ... as these are like a superpower fuel for your amazing body!

BREATHING EXERCISES

You can calm your body and mind by taking big, slow belly breaths! See the Stress-Busting Breathing Exercises later in this book!

EXERCISE

Get your body moving and huffing and puffing! Go for a walk, a run, a bike ride, dance, swim, or skate. This helps burn off that jittery stress energy!

FAVOURITE ACTIVITY

Do something fun and that you love to do! Things like drawing, playing games, making music, building something, or playing dress-ups. This can help change stressful thoughts to happy, fun thoughts.

BE KIND TO YOURSELF

TALK IT OUT

Talk with an adult you trust about the things that make you feel stress. And ask for help if you need it. This helps you realise you are not alone, and that sharing stressful thoughts can make some of them go away.

and ...

GET OUTSiDE

Be in nature - hug a tree, lie on some grass, sit in a park or by the sea or a lake. Notice the things you can see, hear, smell, and feel.

SLEEP WELL

When we sleep our body rests, makes repairs, and makes more energy for the next day - so it is really important to get a good, restful sleep! Every night - do something relaxing before you go to bed, like reading a book, taking a bath, or remembering the best moments of your day. And try to go to bed at the same time every night.

QUiET TiME

Have a peaceful, safe place you can go to if you need a rest or break. Try calming breathing exercises, reading a book, writing your thoughts and feelings in a journal, or making a list of all the things you feel thankful for.

HUG SOMEONE YOU LOVE

Sometimes, a great, big, squishy hug with someone you love can help you feel calm ... and loved!

We can't stop or avoid stressful things happening to us ... but we can learn how to cope with feeling stress!

Stress feels ***really*** uncomfortable because it pushes us out of our **COMFORT ZONE**.

But ... if we manage stress well ... we realise that outside of our comfort zone is often ...

where the magic happens!

Your comfort zone

... is a state of mind where you feel comfortable and safe because you are not being challenged. But this is also a place where you don't learn or grow!

STRESS-BUSTING BREATHING EXERCISES

great for grown-ups too!

Did you know that stress and breathing are closely connected? When we feel stress we ***overbreathe***. In other words, our body automatically starts taking in more air (oxygen) to help our bodies get ready to 'fight or flight' – like if we need to run away from danger, or face a stressful situation. And overbreathing can make us feel more stressed!

The good news is that controlled, mindful breathing exercises lower stress levels and help our bodies and busy minds to feel calm and relaxed.

Here are three easy breathing exercises you can do anywhere, at any time you feel stress ... and try to focus ***only*** on your breathing:

Finger Breathing

This exercise is particularly good for younger children who may have difficulty understanding breath control.

1. Hold one hand in front of you and spread your fingers.
2. Using the index finger (the one you use to point with), ***slowly*** trace the outside of your other hand and fingers.
   Start at the bottom of your thumb and follow it up to the top of the thumb then down the other side.
3. Breathe in through your nose on the way up, and breathe out through your mouth on the way down.
4. Keep tracing all your fingers to your pinkie finger and then back again.
5. Repeat this exercise until you feel calm.
6. Check in with your body, and notice how you feel.

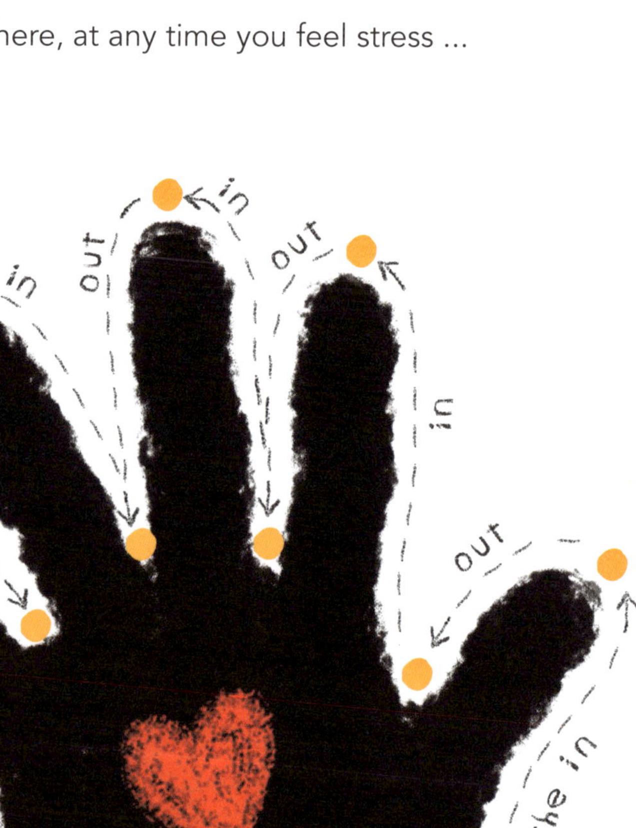

Box Breathing

1. Imagine the 4 sides of a square as you breathe.
2. Side 1: Slowly breathe in through your nose for a count of 4.
3. Side 2: Hold your breath for a count of 4.
4. Side 3: Slowly breathe out through your mouth for a count of 4.
5. Side 4: Hold your breath for a count of 4.
6. Repeat this exercise at least 6 times.
7. Check in with your body, and notice how you feel.

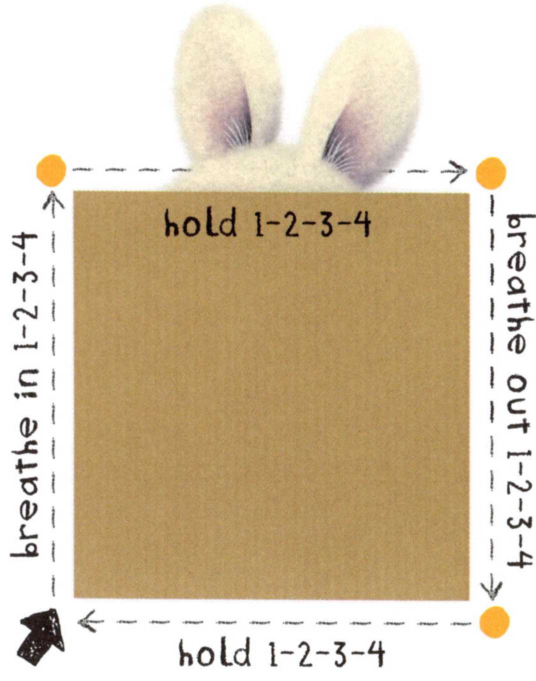

4-7-8 Breathing

This exercise is especially good to acheive deep relaxation or help you fall asleep.

1. Breathe in through your nose for a count of 4 (keeping your mouth closed).
2. Hold your breath for a count of 7.
3. Breathe out through your mouth (like you are blowing a candle out) for a count of 8.
4. Repeat this exercise up to 4 times.
5. Check in with your body, and notice how you feel.

NOTES TO PARENTS AND CAREGIVERS

As busy parents and caregivers, we can easily forget our children feel stress too! There are many things that can cause stress for children such as friendship problems, starting a new school, parents divorcing or separating, the death of a family member, or feeling unsupported. Children do not always have sophisticated language skills to express their needs and feelings, so we need to be highly attuned to their emotional and behavioural cues as their way of communicating with us.

Stress can change how we think, how we behave, and the choices we make, and has a profound effect on our mental and physical wellbeing. It is important to remind your child that stress is normal and we ***all*** experience stress at different times, in varying intensities, about different things. While stress usually goes away quickly after the event (the stressor) has gone – some of us are more naturally predisposed to feeling anxious than others (i.e. a part of a person's personality).

What is Stress?
Stress is a state of physical, mental, or emotional strain or tension resulting from adverse or challenging circumstances. Stress is what we feel when we are worried or uncomfortable about any event or thought, and is our body's reaction to a challenge, pressure, or having to adapt or change.
Stress can be positive in small, short bursts and can provide valuable learning opportunities for children to *practise* dealing with difficult situations at a young age. Each time they manage stress in a healthy way they develop resilience, self-esteem, and self-regulation, and learn essential strategies to enable them to better cope with future challenges.

Conversely, exposing young children to ongoing toxic or chronic stress can affect their brain development, mental and physical wellbeing, and coping ability throughout their lifetime. Chronic stress is stress that lasts for many weeks or months, and continues after the stressor is gone or the stressor is ongoing. Without effective stress management, this may lead to health problems such as high blood pressure, heart disease, depression, and anxiety disorders.

Signs of Stress in Children
Stress in children can cause changes in their typical behaviour and manifest as emotional and physical symptoms described in this book. These feelings and symptoms may be very confusing and uncomfortable for them, so it is important to encourage your child to be in tune with their bodies and recognise how stress feels, label their feelings, and feel comfortable and safe sharing their worries with you.

As parents and caregivers, we need to model good stress management in ourselves, guide our children through the many stress-bumps along the road, and provide them with the skills they need to manage future stress events with greater confidence.

Helping Children Cope With Stress:

Notice when your child is worried about something. Let them know that you have noticed they seem to be worried or bothered, and gently ask them if they would like to talk about it. Show that you care and explain you would like to understand what is worrying them.
If you are aware of a future event or situation that may be stressful for your child – let them know in advance, discuss ways to prepare for it, and let them know that you will support them through it.

Acknowledge your child's feelings – don't dismiss them. Try not to automatically tell your child not to worry, as this may make them feel that feeling stress or worry is wrong. Explain to them that feeling stress is *normal* and is our body's way of telling us to pay attention and be aware of the stressor (the cause of the stress), and that the stressful feelings usually go away after the stressor has gone.

Be a soft place to fall. In other words, actively listen to your child's feelings and concerns *without criticism or judgement*. Try to identify the stressor and talk through different ways your child may like to deal with it and discuss possible outcomes. Giving them age appropriate decisions (along with your loving guidance and support) helps build self-esteem, resilience, and confidence to cope with future stressful events or thoughts. And, sometimes, just talking helps.

Avoid overscheduling. Be mindful not to schedule too many extracurricular activities, or pressure your child to participate and/or succeed. This, in addition to the typical pressure to do well in the school environment, may lead to increased stress and anxiety for your child. Ensure your child has plenty of 'down time' to chill out and relax, to play, and to bond with friends and family.

Healthy living. Sugar, saturated and trans fats (in processed food), and many additives we consume put our bodies under a huge amount of stress, and contribute to the overall stress your child may feel. Ensure your child is getting enough restful sleep, eating healthy food, and drinking lots of water.

Model healthy coping. Your child will learn to model the behaviours they observe in you – including how you manage stress. Talk about some of the things or thoughts that have made you feel stress and how you coped (or not!). Don't be afraid of sharing a stressful situation you didn't manage well – and why – and the things you would do differently. Remember to keep it simple and age appropriate.

Remember: A child who feels loved and supported, and has a sense of their personal abilities and strengths – generally copes with stress well. Regularly reassure your child they are loved, supported, and valued ... simply for being their beautiful self!

For more information and support material visit: **www.tracemoroney.com**

Some of the worst things
in my life
never even happened.

Mark Twain

EQ PUBLICATiONS

Published with love by EQ Publications Ltd
www.eqpublications.nz

www.tracemoroney.com
Edited by Madeleine Collinge

Printed in China by
RR Donnelley Asia Printing Solutions Ltd.

First published 2023.